LIGHT AND COLOUR

Peter Riley

W
FRANKLIN WATTS
LONDON·SYDNEY

This edition 2003

Franklin Watts
96 Leonard Street
London EC2A 4XD

Franklin Watts Australia
45–51 Huntley Street
Alexandria
NSW 2015

© Franklin Watts 1998
Text © Peter Riley 1998

Series editor: Sarah Snashall
Editor: Janet De Saulles
Designer: Mo Choy
Art director: Robert Walster
Picture research: Sue Mennell

Photography: Steve Shott (unless otherwise credited)
Artwork: Peter Bull

A CIP catalogue record for this book is available from the British Library.
Dewey Decimal Classification 535.6

ISBN 0 7496 5212 8

Printed in Belgium

Picture credits:
Bruce Coleman pp. 6b (Kevin Rushby), 20b (Jeff Foott Productions); Eye Ubiquitous pp. 10 (Paul Seheult), 15t (Tim Hawkins), 20t (Paul Thompson); Getty Images pp. 12 (Art Wolfe), 15b (Jeremy Horner); The Golf Picture Library p. 13b (Matthew Harris); Robert Harding p. 25b; Hutchison Library p. 19t; Image Bank pp. 9t, 16; Image Select/Chris Fairclough p. 13t; Images Colour Library pp. 4t, 21, 28b, 29b; NHPA pp. 4b (R. Sorensen & J. Olsen), 5t (Anthony Bannister), 24l (Steve Robinson); Oxford Scientific Films pp. 9b (Edward Robinson), 24r (Max Gibbs), 25t (Michael Fogden), 28t (Michael Leach), 29t (Alistair Shay); Science Photo Library pp. 7t (NASA), 18 (David Parker), 20m (Pekka Parviainen), 22 (Françoise Sauze); The Stock Market p. 19b.

CONTENTS

WHERE LIGHT COMES FROM

The Earth's most powerful natural source of light is the Sun. It provides our planet with vital energy – without it there would be no life on Earth. Other sources of light, such as electric lights, are made by people so that we can see at night or in places where the Sun's light does not reach.

Most of the light on Earth comes from the Sun.

The Moon is the brightest non-luminous object we can see in the sky.

LUMINOUS AND NON-LUMINOUS OBJECTS

Objects that give out light are called luminous objects. The most distant luminous objects are stars which are millions of kilometres away.

Most objects, however, are non-luminous – they do not give out light. We can only see them because luminous objects shine on them, and they reflect enough light to enable us to see them. Some objects reflect so much light, they shine. The Moon reflects the light of the Sun onto the Earth at night.

Natural light sources

While the powerful natural light of the Sun gives light and energy to the Earth, other smaller natural light sources are found on the Earth itself. Glow worms send out light through the trees and, during storms, flashes of lightning brighten the dark skies for a moment. Even in the darkness of the deep ocean there are fish which give out light from spots on their bodies.

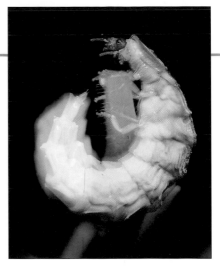

Female glow worms give off light from the ends of their bodies to attract a mate.

Artificial light sources

When people first discovered how to make fire, they discovered how to light up the dark as well as how to keep warm. Today, inventions such as candles, torches, lamps and television or computer screens give out light, and make our lives easier and more enjoyable.

■ INVESTIGATE!

Make a list of all the light sources around you. How many are natural and how many have been made by people?

A candle allows us to see at night when the Sun's light does not reach us.

LIGHT ON THE MOVE

Light travels from its source to the object it is lighting. It moves in a straight line and travels faster than anything else we know about. The energy in a light ray can be used by us to power instruments such as calculators.

This calculator is powered by energy from the Sun.

SPEED OF LIGHT

Light travels at 300,000 kilometres per second. The Sun is so far away that, even at this speed, its light takes eight minutes to reach Earth. If you are reading this book in daylight, the light reaching you now left the Sun eight minutes ago.

Light from a lamp travels at the same speed, but because it only has to travel a tiny distance to reach you, it seems to light up where you are instantly.

Can you see the straight edges to these sunbeams?

SUNBEAMS

You can see how light travels in a straight line by looking at rays of sunlight shining through a gap in the clouds. The rays take the form of sunbeams which pass through the air to the ground. The particles of dust in the air shine in the beam, showing us exactly where the light is travelling.

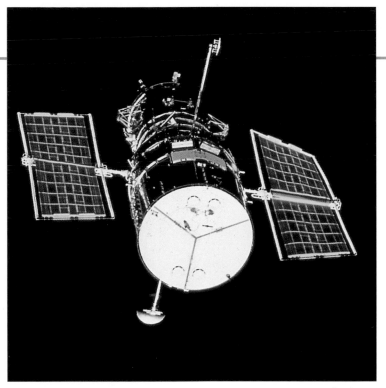

LIGHT ENERGY

The energy in light can be changed into other forms of energy. Solar cells on a calculator or solar panels on a satellite change the light energy into electrical energy. Green plants trap light energy in their leaves and use it to make food.

Solar panels on the Hubble space telescope mean that the telescope does not need to carry large and heavy supplies of fuel.

Green plants use some of the energy in light to make food.

■ INVESTIGATE!

See how light travels in straight lines by shining a torch through a comb.

LIGHT AND MATERIALS

When a ray of light hits an object, the light may pass through the object, be reflected or be soaked up (absorbed). What happens to the light depends on the type of material it strikes.

TRANSPARENT MATERIALS

Some materials, such as glass, clear plastic and water, let rays of light pass straight through them. These materials are called transparent materials. A small amount of the light striking such materials, however, is reflected. This is useful to us, since it shows us the position of the surface of the material.

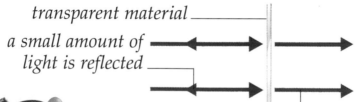

transparent material

a small amount of light is reflected

light rays passing through

Because this jar is made from clear glass, it is easy to see the sweets inside it.

TRANSLUCENT MATERIALS

A few materials, such as tissue paper, let light pass through them, but scatter the rays in all directions. Some kinds of glass are made translucent by being given a rough surface.

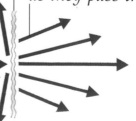

translucent material

some of the light rays are reflected back

some light rays scatter as they pass through

We can only get an impression of the colours and shapes of the sweets inside this translucent glass goblet.

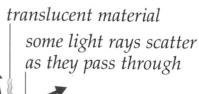

OPAQUE MATERIALS

Materials such wood and brick do not let any light pass through them. They are called opaque materials. They soak up most of the light which reaches them. The small amount of light which they reflect allows us to see them.

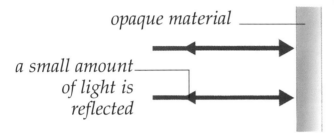

opaque material

a small amount of light is reflected

The inside of this tunnel is in darkness because light cannot pass through the solid rock of the hill.

The mist in the air scatters the Sun's light rays in many directions, making it difficult to see the landscape clearly.

INVESTIGATE!

Shine a torch on various objects around your home. Make a list of all the transparent, translucent and opaque objects you find. Were you surprised by any of your discoveries?

SHADOWS

Light rays shining onto one side of an opaque object are absorbed or reflected. They cannot pass through the object and light up the area on the other side. A shadow forms behind the object.

Shadows can make interesting patterns.

HOW SHADOWS ARE FORMED

The light rays which pass by the sides of the object keep moving in a straight line. They cannot bend round the side and fill the area behind the object with light. The area on the unlit side is in darkness because no light can enter it.

THE SIZE AND SHAPE OF A SHADOW

If an object is moved round in the light, different parts of it stop the light rays and the shape of the shadow changes.

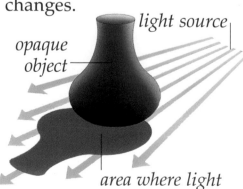

light source

opaque object

area where light rays cannot reach

HIGH AND LOW SOURCES OF LIGHT

At midday, when the Sun is high in the sky, shadows of people and buildings are very short. At the beginning or end of the day, though, when the Sun is low in the sky, the shadows are long.

The shadow of this pineapple is short because the light is high above it.

The shadow of this apple is long because the light source is low down.

LIGHT FROM FAR AND NEAR

An opaque object blocks many of the light rays coming from the surface of a distant light source such as the Sun. This makes a shadow with a very clear edge.

INVESTIGATE!

Shine a torch on an object from different angles and heights and from near and far. What happens to the shape of the shadow?

An object cannot block so many of the light rays coming from the surface of a close light source, such as a reading lamp. This makes a dark shadow with a lighter edge. The dark part of the shadow is called the umbra and the lighter part is called the penumbra.

The light source is near to this apple and so the shadow is clearly made up of an umbra and penumbra.

FLAT MIRRORS

When light strikes a mirror, most of the light is reflected. This makes a picture in the mirror called an image.

HOW A MIRROR WORKS

The light rays in a beam of light travel in parallel lines. When they strike a smooth surface, they are reflected in the parallel lines. This arrangement of the light rays lets you see an image of where they came from in the surface of a flat mirror. Because the metal coating behind the mirror absorbs very little light, most of the rays are reflected. This makes the image bright and easy to see.

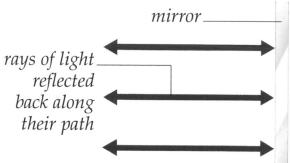

mirror

rays of light reflected back along their path

Light rays are reflected by a flat mirror back along their paths. This lets you see an image of where they came from in the surface of the mirror.

NATURE'S MIRRORS

Other flat, shiny surfaces which reflect light well include water and polished metals. If you look into them, you may see a reflection of yourself in just the same way that you can see an image of yourself when you look into a mirror.

Still water makes an excellent 'natural' mirror.

WRONG WAY ROUND

If you stand in front of a mirror, the light rays from your face strike the mirror head on at 90° to the surface. The rays are reflected back along the path they came. The light from the right hand side of your face makes the left hand side of the face in your image. This means that the image in the mirror is reversed.

Can you see how this boy's right hand becomes his left hand in the mirror's reflection?

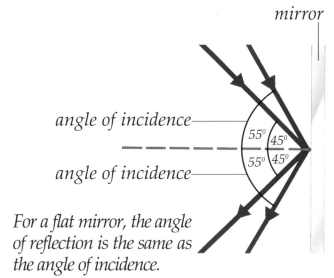

mirror

angle of incidence

55° 45°
55° 45°

angle of incidence

For a flat mirror, the angle of reflection is the same as the angle of incidence.

REFLECTING A LIGHT BEAM

If a beam of light is shone from a torch onto a flat mirror at an angle, it is reflected from the mirror at the same angle. The angle at which the beam strikes the mirror's surface is called the angle of incidence. The angle at which the reflected ray leaves the surface is called the angle of reflection.

■ INVESTIGATE!

Shine a torch through the teeth of a comb at a flat mirror. First shine the torch straight onto the mirror. Next change the angle at which the light shines on the mirror. What happens to the path of the reflected light?

In a periscope, light is reflected through two mirrors so a person can see over a wall or a crowd of people.

CURVED MIRRORS

Some shiny surfaces are not flat. They still reflect light to make an image, but the images they make are different sizes from the object.

path of light rays — *concave mirror*

light rays converge

Light rays hitting the surface of a concave mirror are reflected inwards.

CONCAVE MIRRORS

When a shiny surface bends inwards, it makes a concave mirror. If you look in a concave mirror from a long way off, your image is small and upside down. If you move very close to the mirror, your image is magnified and the right way up. Concave mirrors are used for shaving and make-up mirrors. When a person puts their face close to the mirror, they can see a magnified view of their skin.

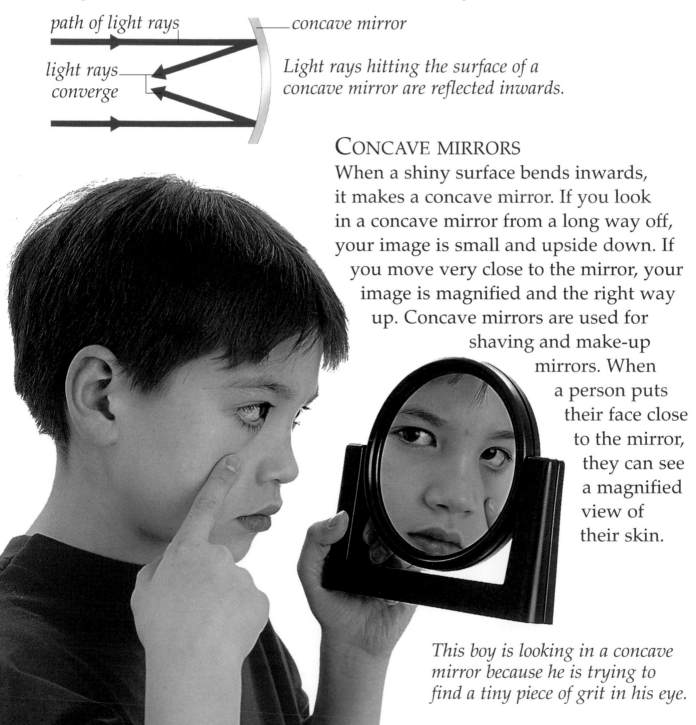

This boy is looking in a concave mirror because he is trying to find a tiny piece of grit in his eye.

CONVEX MIRRORS

When a shiny surface bends outwards, it makes a convex mirror. When you look in a convex mirror from any distance, your image is always small, but it is always the right way up.

light rays diverge

convex mirror

path of light rays

Light rays hitting the surface of a convex mirror are reflected outwards.

A convex mirror gives a wide view of the surroundings, and helps drivers to see buildings or traffic all around them.

At some fun fairs, concave and convex mirrors are put together to give you strange images.

■ INVESTIGATE!

Use the inside of a spoon as a concave mirror and the outside as a convex mirror. What are the images like?

BENDING LIGHT RAYS

Some light rays bend when they move from one transparent material to another. This bending is called refraction.

WHY LIGHT RAYS BEND
Light travels at different speeds in different transparent materials. When a light ray passes from one transparent material, such as air, to a second transparent material, such as glass, it changes speed.

If the light ray meets the surface of the second material head on at right angles to it, the ray passes straight through and does not bend. If the light ray meets the surface between the materials at an angle, the change in speed makes the ray change direction and the light ray is bent.

A light ray bends as it enters a glass block, then bends again at the same angle as it leaves.

STANDING IN WATER
If you stand in the water in a swimming pool and look down at your feet, your legs seem to be shorter than they really are. The light rays coming from your feet bend when they enter the air and look as if they come from another place near the surface. This makes your feet appear closer and your legs seem shorter.

The parts of this mother and child which are under water appear to be closer than they really are. This is because the light rays bend between the water and the air.

LENSES

A lens is a transparent piece of glass or plastic. It has opposite sides which are curved. A lens with two sides curved outwards is called a biconvex lens. A lens with two sides curved inwards is called a biconcave lens.

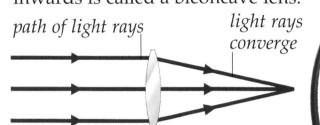

path of light rays

light rays converge

A biconvex lens bends light rays to make a magnified image when you hold it close to an object and look through it.

path of light rays

light rays diverge

A biconcave lens bends light to make a smaller image of an object.

A magnifying glass is made from a biconvex lens. Can you see how it enlarges the detail of this leaf?

INVESTIGATE!

Fill a plastic bottle with water and shine rays of light through it from a torch and comb. Squeeze the bottle. What happens to the rays of light?

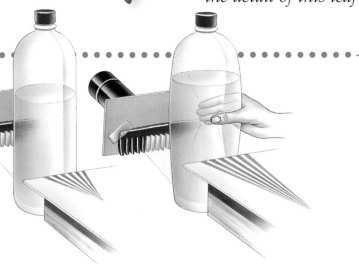

COLOUR IN LIGHT

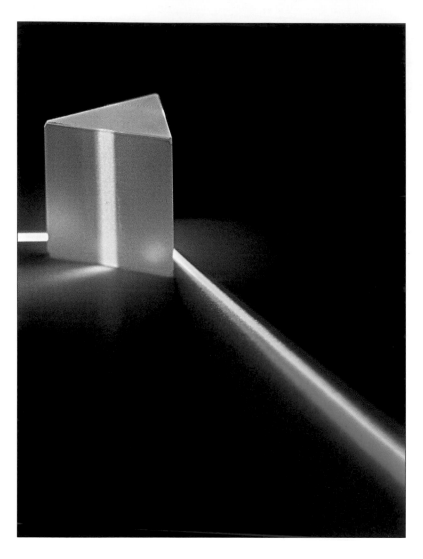

A ray of light from the Sun is made up of seven different colours visible to the naked eye. Together, these seven colours are known as a spectrum. It is these colours in light which give colour to everything around us.

Part of this beam of white light is reflected off the prism. The remaining part of the beam is split into a spectrum.

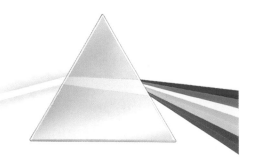

The colours in light separate as they pass through a prism because each colour of the spectrum is refracted a different amount.

SPLITTING UP THE COLOURS

If a ray of light strikes the side of a prism at an angle, it is bent or refracted as it goes into the glass. The ray travels through the prism until it strikes the other side where it is bent again as it passes into the air. The change in speed as the light goes through the prism and out again makes light separate into the seven colours of the spectrum – red, orange, yellow, green, blue, indigo and violet.

THE COLOURS OF AN OBJECT

When sunlight shines on something, some colours are absorbed and some are reflected. The reflected light gives the object its colour. A red object absorbs six colours but reflects the red light. A green object absorbs six colours but reflects the green light. A white object reflects all seven colours. A black object, on the other hand, absorbs all seven colours and so appears black.

The threads in this colourful clothing reflect a wide range of colours.

Light filters are used with stage lights to make special effects for this concert.

A LIGHT FILTER

A light filter is made from a piece of transparent – but coloured – glass or plastic. It absorbs some of the colours of light but lets others pass through it. A red filter, for example, absorbs six colours and lets the red light pass through.

▌INVESTIGATE!

Make a slit in a piece of black card, stick the card to a jar filled with water, and let the sunlight shine through the water then through the slit. Can you see the spectrum of colours that forms?

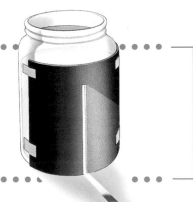

Colours in the Sky

The sky is sometimes full of wonderful colours. This is because the gases around the Earth – the Earth's atmosphere – can split light up into its various colours.

Sky colours

In the day, dust particles and water droplets in the atmosphere scatter the colours in sunlight. Of all the colours in light, blue is scattered the most, and this makes the sky blue.

Night time

The night sky is dark when the part of the Earth below it has turned away from the Sun and is in shadow. The Moon beams down a strong, steady, reflected light to the ground. The weak light from distant stars is refracted by the air moving through the atmosphere, making them appear to twinkle.

Sun colours

When the Sun is near the horizon, its light shines through a thicker layer of the atmosphere than at midday. This scatters the yellow light, leaving red and orange to shine directly from the Sun at sunrise and sunset. At midday the Sun is overhead. Its light passes through a thinner layer of the atmosphere, so the yellow light does not scatter.

CLOUDS

Clouds are made from billions of tiny water droplets close together. Sunlight can shine through a cloud, but its light is scattered in all directions as it is reflected off the water droplets. This scattering of light makes the clouds white.

In a rain cloud there are so many raindrops that they absorb more light than they reflect, and so the cloud appears grey.

◼ INVESTIGATE!

Put a few drops of milk in a transparent bowl full of water. Stir them up and shine a torch through the bowl. Look for the milk particles scattering the light, making the water appear slightly blue.

RAINBOW

When you watch rain falling, if the Sun is shining from behind you, you may see how the raindrops act as prisms and make a rainbow.

Raindrops can split sunlight up into its seven different colours, creating wonderful rainbows.

MIXING COLOUR

There are three colours of light and three colours of paint which are each called the primary colours. The primary colours of light are red, green and blue. The primary colours of paint are yellow, cyan (blue) and magenta (bright pink).

Where all three primary colours of light overlap, white light is formed.

MIXING COLOURED LIGHT

The three primary colours of light can be used to make light of many different colours. If red and green light are mixed, yellow is made. Blue and red light together produce magenta, and green and blue make cyan.

COLOUR TELEVISION

On a colour television screen, there are strips of chemicals called phosphors. The phosphors are red, green or blue and each one glows to make all the colours that are needed. For example, brown is made when green phosphors glow brightly and red phosphors glow dimly.

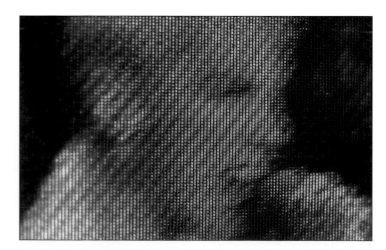

Each coloured phosphor on a TV screen can glow a different brightness from the others to create all the colours around us.

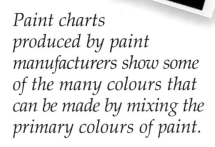

MIXING COLOURED PAINT

The colour in paint is made by small solid particles called pigments. They are spread out through the liquid part of the paint. Each pigment absorbs some colours in sunlight and reflects others.

The three primary coloured pigments of yellow, cyan and magenta can be used to make many other different colours. For example, when yellow and cyan pigments are mixed together, they absorb all the colours from each other except green, so this is the colour of the paint they make.

Paint charts produced by paint manufacturers show some of the many colours that can be made by mixing the primary colours of paint.

As the water mixes with the red ink on this piece of blotting paper, the dyes start to separate.

THE COLOURS IN INK

Some inks are made from mixtures of different coloured dyes. The dyes can be seen by placing a drop of ink on filter paper and putting drops of water on it.

■ INVESTIGATE!

Make an ink spot on a piece of filter paper and add drops of water to it. What colours do you see as the ink spreads out?

COLOURS IN ANIMALS

Some animals have amazingly colourful bodies. These colours serve useful purposes, helping them to hide, to find a mate or to warn other animals of their presence.

A peacock displays his colourful feathers in order to attract a partner.

COLOURS FOR DISPLAY

The males of some kinds of animals are brightly coloured in order to attract a mate for breeding. The male guppy displays his beautiful colours by swimming in front of the female. In the same way, the males of many kinds of birds are extravagantly coloured. They use their colours, their songs and their movements to attract a mate.

This male guppy swims past the female fish, finding a mate by displaying his bright colours.

COLOURS FOR WARNING

Some animals are poisonous if they are eaten. They have bright colours to warn predators not to eat them. Many caterpillars are safe from insect-eating animals because the animals recognise their colourful warning signals. A young animal may attack a poisonous caterpillar but spit it out when it tastes the poison. The animal quickly learns not to try and feed on that type of caterpillar again.

This poisonous caterpillar looks deadly and tastes deadly too!

HIDING AWAY

Most animals use colours to camouflage their bodies and hide from predators. Their bodies may be just one colour, for example the brown coat of a deer helps the animal hide in the trees of a wood or forest.

Some animals, such as some frogs, use blotches of different colours to help break up the outline of their bodies. This makes them more difficult to see.

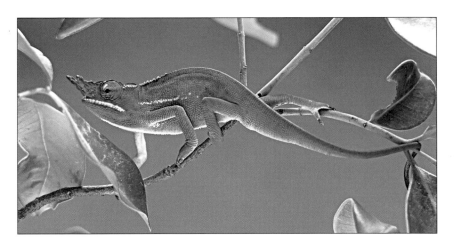

Chameleons change colour to match their surroundings. This chameleon has become green to match the leaves it is crawling among.

■ INVESTIGATE!

Look at an area of grass, soil and stones and make a drawing of a local animal. Paint the animal in colours that would camouflage it in the area you have chosen.

THE EYE

We are able to see things because light rays coming from them pass through the air and enter our eyes. There are many parts to the eye which help us to see.

iris

pupil

white of the eye

OUTSIDE THE EYE

Most of the outside of the eye is covered in a white coat, but the front part of the eye is transparent. This part is called the cornea. Behind the cornea is a transparent liquid, and behind this is a coloured ring of muscles called the iris. The iris surrounds a black hole called the pupil. Light rays travel through the cornea and liquid, entering the eye through the pupil.

The eye's iris may be brown, blue or shades of bluey-grey or green. This does not affect the colours a person sees.

INSIDE THE EYE

Behind the pupil is a lens. It can change its shape and bend light rays so that they can make a picture inside the eye. After the light rays have passed through the lens, they move through a transparent jelly to the inside wall of the eye, or retina.

Here, the light rays form an upside down image of the place the eye is looking at. The retina sends details of this image along nerves to the brain, which turns the image the right way up, allowing us to see.

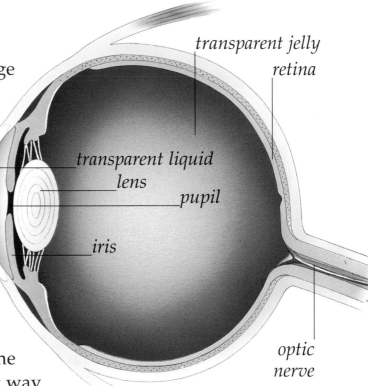

transparent jelly

retina

transparent liquid

lens

pupil

cornea

iris

optic nerve

The inside of the eye.

Some people wear glasses to correct their eyesight.

GLASSES AND CONTACT LENSES

The lenses in some people's eyes bend the light rays too little or too much, making a blurred image on their retinas. Glasses or contact lenses bend the light in the opposite way to the lenses in these people's eyes so that they can see clearly.

■ INVESTIGATE!

The eyelids blink to clean the front of the eye. How many times do you blink in a minute?

ANIMAL EYES

A nimals have different types of eyes, depending on whether they are hunters who are looking for prey, or prey who have to watch out for attackers.

An owl has forward-facing eyes so that it can judge how far away its prey is.

JUDGING DISTANCES

Each eye is able to see a certain area around it. This is called its field of view. If two eyes face in the same direction, like humans' eyes do, the fields of view overlap. This lets the animal judge distances well. Animals with eyes that face forwards are predators. They can judge the distance of their prey before they attack, helping them to catch the animal quickly.

SEEING ALL AROUND

Animals such as deer and rabbits have eyes which face in different directions. Each eye sticks out a little to give it a very wide field of view. If a rabbit had its eyes facing forwards, it would not see its attackers creep up behind it.

The eyes are on opposite sides of the deer's head to let it see all around, allowing it to keep watch for predators.

Dragonflies have large numbers of small eyes to give them a wide field of view, helping them to catch insects in flight.

INSECT EYES

The top of an insect eye looks like a honeycomb. It is made up of lots of tiny eyes. Each tiny eye makes an image which is linked to the images from the other eyes. The final image is made up in much the same way as the picture of a completed jigsaw puzzle.

■ INVESTIGATE!

Put a pen and its top on a table. Close one eye and quickly pick them up and put the top on the pen. How many goes does it take? Try again using both eyes.

Because frogs spend so much of their time in the water, their eyes are on the top of their heads — they can stay safely underwater yet look out around them.

GLOSSARY

ANGLE OF INCIDENCE – the angle at which a light ray strikes a mirror.

ANGLE OF REFLECTION – the angle at which a light ray is reflected away from the surface of a mirror.

ATMOSPHERE – the layer of gases which we call the air and which covers the surface of the Earth.

BICONCAVE LENS – a lens with two surfaces curved inwards.

BICONVEX LENS – a lens with two surfaces curved outwards.

CATERPILLAR – a stage in the life cycle of butterflies and moths.

CONCAVE MIRROR – a mirror which has a surface that curves inwards.

CONVERGE – when light rays coming from different directions meet at the same point.

CONVEX MIRROR – a mirror which has a surface that curves outwards.

CORNEA – the transparent front part of the eye.

DIVERGE – when light rays separate and go in different directions.

GLOW WORM – a kind of beetle which has luminous parts to its body.

HORIZON – the place where the sky appears to meet the Earth's surface.

HUBBLE SPACE TELESCOPE – a giant telescope moving in an orbit around the Earth and which is used to study the universe.

IMAGE – a picture seen in a mirror or made by a lens focusing light.

INSECT – an animal with six legs and usually two pairs of wings.

IRIS – the coloured part of the eye.

LENS – a piece of transparent material used to alter the path of rays of light passing though it.

LIGHT FILTER – a piece of coloured glass or plastic which lets light of one colour pass through it.

LUMINOUS OBJECT – an object which gives out light, for example the Sun or an electric light-bulb.

MAGNIFIED IMAGE – an image which appears larger than the object from which it is made.

NON-LUMINOUS OBJECT – an object which does not give out light. It is seen because of the light that it reflects from its surface.

OPAQUE MATERIAL – a material through which light cannot pass.

PARALLEL LINES – lines which lie next to each other and which are the same distance from each other all the way along their length.

PENUMBRA – the light grey edge to a shadow.

PERISCOPE – a device in which light is reflected by mirrors so a person can see around a corner or over a high wall.

PHOSPHORS – chemicals used in the production of television screens and which can produce light.

PIGMENT – a material which gives colour to a paint.

PREDATOR – an animal that feeds on other animals.

PREY – an animal which is eaten by other animals.

PRISM – a block of glass with a triangular shape.

PUPIL – the black hole at the centre of the iris in the eye.

RAINBOW – the spectrum produced in the sky when light shines through raindrops.

REFLECTION – a picture of a scene or object seen on a smooth surface such as a mirror or on calm water.

REFRACTION – a process in which the path of a ray of light is changed as it passes through a transparent material.

RETINA – the part of the eye which is sensitive to light.

SATELLITE – a machine which moves around the Earth in space.

SHADOW – the dark area behind an object where rays from a light source cannot reach.

SOLAR CELL – a device which changes some of the energy shining on to it into electrical energy and which then makes a current of electricity.

SOLAR PANEL – a structure made up of a number of solar cells.

SPECTRUM – a band of seven colours that make up white light. The colours are red, orange, yellow, green, blue, indigo and violet.

TRANSLUCENT MATERIAL – a material through which some light passes but which does not allow objects on the other side to be clearly seen.

TRANSPARENT MATERIAL – a material through which light passes and which allows objects on the other side to be clearly seen.

UMBRA – the darkest part of a shadow which lies inside the lighter penumbra.

INDEX